HIT AND MISS

LEONARD STANLEY C.E. (AIDED) PRIMARY SCHOOL
BATH ROAD
LEONARD STANLEY
STONEHOUSE
GLOUCESTERSHIRE   GL10 3LY

Written by Tony Bradman
Illustrated by Steve Stone

"I'm bored, Mum," moaned Robin. "Bored, bored, BORED."

"I know. You keep getting under my feet!" sighed Mum. "Off you go into town. I want you to do some shopping."

"Do I have to?" moaned Robin.
Mum just gave him a look.

Robin trudged off towards the town. The market was very crowded when he got there, with lots of pushing and shoving.

"I *hate* shopping," Robin muttered. Suddenly he heard cheering, and went to see what was going on.

Robin crept to the front of the crowd. Some targets had been set up on the green for an archery contest.

All the archers were good, but one man was better than the rest. Robin watched. He had never seen anything so exciting.

Robin crept up to take a closer look. He wished he had a bow and arrows too.

"That would be so cool," he whispered to himself.

Then he had an idea – and ran home as fast as he could go.

Strange noises came from the little shed
– **BANG, BANG ... TWANG!**
"What are you doing, Robin?" Mum asked.

Robin came out at last.

"I've been making these," he said. "What do you think?"

"Not a lot," said Mum, with a frown.

Robin wasn't bored any more – he was having a great time, but Rufus the cat wasn't.

"Stop!" yelled Mum. "Those arrows are dangerous!"

Mum said Robin had to make them safe. He put corks on them ...

... but they made the arrows heavy. He missed what he was trying to hit, and hit things he should have missed. He broke quite a few things as well.

"Right, that's enough!"
Mum snapped at last.
"Give me those arrows!"
Robin handed them over
... and sulked.

Robin was more bored than ever now. He moaned and groaned and sulked and sighed. Mum sighed too. "What am I going to do with you?" she said.

Later, she had an idea ...

"Come on Robin, we're going out," said Mum.

"Great!" said Robin. He cheered up immediately. "Where to?"

"Oh, I just want to do a bit of shopping," Mum replied.

"Oh no! Not again! You know I *hate* shopping," moaned Robin.

Mum smiled.

Robin trudged into town behind Mum. They stopped at a shop – and he could hardly believe what happened next.

Mum bought him a proper bow and arrows!
"Wow! Thanks, Mum!" he said.
"But there *is* just one thing," said Mum.

"You will have to take lessons! That way I know we'll all be safe."

"No problem, Mum," said Robin. "I would love to!"

So young Robin Hood started learning how to use a bow. He wasn't very good at first ...

... but he got better. In fact, it wasn't long before he was very good indeed!